Systematic Desensitization

The Adventure of a

Lifetime

Chris Vernet

Manufactured in the United States of America

ISBN-13: 978-1098855109 | **ISBN-10**: 1098855108

Acknowledgements

"There's more to a book than meets the eye.

Everyone's life is a book, READ IT!"

- Chris Vernet

It would have me lose sleep at night to not give thanks to each and every person I have known and met, as well as for the loving people that I have yet been blessed to meet. I would like to acknowledge each and every person on this beautiful planet, especially you who is reading this. For if it weren't for you, this book would not have the ability to produce life. A very special thank you goes out to my loving mother for giving me the gift of unconditional love. I want to also send a special thank you to my Godmother, Dr. McKellar for giving me a plethora of blessings throughout my life, and providing me the chance to have opportunities that others dream of. Other blessings in my life that have brought this idea to life include Dr.

Taglialatela, my senior year college professor, who inspired me to think big and dig deep towards what I believe could bring the most benefit and growth to our world. Last and certainly not least, I would like to thank the Apple of my Eye, Bonita, who inspired and supported my writing.

Pit Stops

- Preparation For The Adventure

- The Calming Before the Storm

- Freeing Yourself From The System

- The System

- Systematic Desensitization

Preparation For The Adventure

"One question always leads to another. Some things are better to wonder about"

- Christopher Pike

Have your eyes ever been bigger than your stomach, and you ordered or made too much food? Have you ever wanted that small, last bite to fill you all the way up? Have you ever indulged in just the right amount, and best tasting food that you felt as if you not only had the best meal of your life, it was also the most fulfilling? The hope and aspiration of this adventure are just as that last question; to provide for you that beautiful feeling of fulfillment. Joy comes from giving you the read that not only you desire, this read is to be one of the most fulfilling you've ever had. In reading this book, you are about to go on the adventure of a lifetime! Before going on this adventure, you must know I appreciate you taking the time to go on it. In preparation for this adventure, all that is suggested is to remember to take moments to yourself throughout the adventure to appreciate our journey to the fullest. * marks have been placed as a friendly reminder for highly suggested breaks. Where the * marks are placed, there is also a full blank page for you to take notes, write down your thoughts, and give you something to look back on in reflection of your growth process. This is important because we currently live in a world where many people don't truly appreciate the journey of their adventure. A majority of people focus and see only the small picture, and do not focus on the big picture. The people that use this type of focus use it because of the system we live in. That is why this adventure has been coined 'Systematic Desensitization'. From personal experiences, it has been learned that some of the most fulfilling experiences in life such as the one you will feel after going on this adventure are usually experienced after a journey. Examples include a long hour and half hike in 4 inches of snow to arrive to a beautiful set of hot springs, reaching a fitness goal after strenuous weeks of blood, sweat, tears, and dieting, or marriage and finding your soulmate after spending time being single. It's interesting and necessary to think about marriage because it's a large part of the system we live in, and happens on a regular basis, yet specifically in regards to the states, we have an extremely high divorce rate. Have you ever wondered why that is? Before going deep into marriage, regardless if you are married or not, take one of those brief moments and reflect to yourself what marriage is to you, and what it means.

What came to light with this reflection? Now, that you have your answer, ask yourself if it is your answer and what you believe, or is that what you have been lead or taught to believe? Take a second, and dig deep before coming to the conclusion. The reason to think about how you personally feel about it is because people tend to have a perception of what marriage is based from what they see on T.V., what they see in their families, as well as what they hear or see from others. When it comes to these different sources regarding the concept of marriage, it brings up the question if people truly understand what marriage is with so many different perceptions and versions of it. Are marriages all the same, or are they all different? If they are all the same, why are they different? If they are all different, why does marriage have one word to describe the experience? When it comes to marriage, some loving and lasting marriages begin as two people dating. There are those sleeper ones in which the couple starts out as friends. There are also the sudden ones that meet, fall in love, get married within three months, and still have a happy marriage. Seeing two people conjoin their lives, synchronize each other's hearts, creating one of

the most harmonious relationships man knows of is a

beautiful thing. Before getting to that point of saying I do,

there was a journey that the couple took to make it that far.

Whether it was the journey of multiple dates to find out if

they were the most optimal fit for each other and later felt

nothing but blessed in each other's company; living

together, and finding out who their loved one is behind

closed doors; going from the friend zone to the I want to

be with you forever zone; living such a life that the couple

knew within three months they wanted to be together for

the rest of their lives; there was and is always a journey.

There were most likely moments in the couple's journey in

which they felt they were at the top of the world, such as

that present moment of looking into each other's soul at

the altar. There were most likely moments when they

believed they were at the lowest point in their relationship (that brief moment in which they thought their relationship was over). Let's take it a level deeper, and think about the outside relationships. The people invited to the wedding and those attending the ceremony are most likely the most influential people in the couple's lives. These are the same people that played a part in shaping the couple's beliefs and lives, magically bringing the two lovebirds together. One of the people attending the wedding is the one that introduced the couple. Don't forget about the people who weren't invited to the wedding, that also had an influence in both the lover's lives. If it hadn't been for the bride's terrible relationship with her ex, she would've never been able to separate herself from a damaging relationship in order to find the most empowering relationship she's ever known. The best man in the wedding became the best man after a single moment over ten years before the wedding day. In that moment, the best man asked the groom if he needed a ride home after high school football practice because the groom's mother could not pick him up. The groom appreciated the offer so much that an unbreakable connection was created. These are the journeys that occurred creating the adventure, event, experience, or ceremony of a wedding. These are the journeys that people tend to forget or not appreciate during the moment. When looking deeper and wider into the adventure of a wedding, and being able to see the big picture. All the people involved in the ceremony from the groomsmen and bridesmaids to the servers at the open bar, they are not only all connected, everyone is a working factor in the product of the couple's commitment to creating harmony. This is an example of moving one's thought process towards the bigger picture rather than just looking at the wedding photos and thinking "oh, how wonderful and cute", or just attending the wedding to drink at the open bar. To actually see it, understand how it all came together, what is truly being created in the celebration of love is such a beautiful thing that can bring tears of joy to the eyes. Without the creation of harmony or connecting the whole, the result is incompleteness. This is why a marriage is so significant. That which is broken becomes unbroken. Before we start tearing up at the thought of this beautiful moment, think about one of the best things you've ever experienced (outside of getting married if you are married). Write that experience down. If the water works have started to flow, it brings happiness that tears of joy have been brought to your eyes.

Now that you have the experience written down. How long did it take you to bring that experience back to mind? Did you give it your full attention, focus, and think about the details of that experience as to why it is one of the best? How long did bringing the details to life take for you? How often do you think about this experience? How often do you celebrate it? The idea is not to reminisce or be stuck in the past, the idea is to elevate the spirit. The reason we begin to play twenty-one questions is because a majority of people do not resonate with, or celebrate the most positive experiences of their life for an extended period of time. Many resonate with the negative ones, and let those affect them for an extended period of time. For example, when someone receives a job promotion, they are usually excited. How long are they excited, or how long is the promotion celebrated? Maybe a few hours, a couple of days, maybe even a month; they then forget about it, and get back to work. This same person that received the job promotion was scolded by their parents, teachers, or peers as a child, and years later is psychologically dependent on the praise of their parents, bosses, or co-workers. They are dependent and scarred until reopening that wound in order to heal, or until death. Events of this nurture occur consciously, and subconsciously. Have you ever thought about something like this? How something positive in life happens for you, and how long you remember it versus how something negative happens for you, and how long you remember that. To reiterate, everything in life does happen for you, and not to you. Life gives you the double-edged sword, so that you may learn to wield the most powerful gift offered. Events occur, and not all are remembered. The ones that can easily fade away or become clouded are the ones during childhood. Something very interesting is during a human beings youth, they are the human sponge. During the youth phase is when the identity of a human is largely shaped. At youth, humans are living forms of clay that can be molded to what society deems fit. Before focusing on that topic, there are scientific studies that suggest people can't remember key events because they're such a negative experience that the person buries it deep into their subconscious. This is a known act called repression. Continuing on this rollercoaster, let's get back to that most amazing experience you've ever experienced. There are trillions of different types of experiences that you, your friends, and loved ones thought about when asked that question. It could've been that huge game that you, or your favorite team won; maybe it was your first kiss; when you received your first car; it might've been your first concert. The perfect example of the best experience that can be thought of is **LIFE**. Think about it for just a moment. Would you have had that ultimate experience if you weren't born and alive? Let's take the example of someone's birthday: a person's birthday, or the day their life was created is celebrated for **ONE** day. This celebration can occur by themselves, hopefully with others, or unfortunately is sometimes not celebrated at all. Before and after that day, outside of the few outliers of our world, it's as if the world feels that person doesn't deserve gifts, attention, or love. The result of this kind of experience creates a person who doesn't receive external gifts or praise, before or after the day they were born until their next birthday. It then seems as if the person internally forgets about what they deserve on a daily basis, and they also forget about the best experience they've had and are currently living; life. This much occuring practice in a sense subliminally disempowers people in the world causing them to not value themselves. This is not only seen in the most important experience you've ever had, the day you were born. If we start to expand our view on the larger picture, it is seen on other days such as Christmas, Halloween, Mother's Day, or even Sunday. Have you ever wondered why some people love, and want to treat their mother the way mom's need to always be treated on Mother's day, or why it's okay to be Christian only on the day you're told to go to church? Superficially generalizing, yet as we continue to go deeper, one could begin to think about what is at play. A challenge set forth is to listen to your heart, find what is truly important to you, and celebrate life everyday with your actions. What is it that you live for on a daily basis? Is it to survive, or is it to thrive? Do you live for others, or do you live for yourself?

Can we thrive on our own, and can we truly live without others? Earlier you wrote down your best experience that you've ever experienced; it forever is and will be not only beautiful, but also an important one. Within your mind, bring that experience back to life, and think about everything that led up to that experience. That's the journey! That's what many people always forget to appreciate and be grateful for, and that is life! Many will always appreciate those great experiences yet most forget or want to forget all that happened before it, and will most likely forget that great experience after a short period of time. The games you lost, or watched your favorite team lose before that big win; the years you had to hitch rides, and wait before getting behind your own set of wheels. The journey is what brought you to that experience, and made it that much more fulfilling. When the new season comes, is that big game still celebrated, and after you've had your car for 6 years, is it still your baby? Take a brief moment to ask yourself when you're journeying, if you appreciate it and are you grateful for what it is. Ask yourself if you understand that the moment will pass, yet can always be celebrated through your expression of living. If your tendency is to do so, congratulations, you are ahead of the game. If you don't, that is okay, you were taught to be that way. This guide was created to help you out of that way of living. If you're currently lost right now, and it still hasn't hit home for you; visualize the experience of receiving funds in your bank account for extremely hard work you did. Ask yourself: does receiving those funds feel like a more fulfilling experience to you than the work you did to receive it? Most people are more fulfilled with just having the income, hence why many are no longer passionate about their work. It's these types of experiences and mindsets that cause people to be blind to the most important things in life. The mindset and experiences themselves are systematically created to blind people, and lead people to live unfulfilling and string tied lives. Does the system do it on purpose, or did it happen by accident? This is something that's discussed later.

Everything being said, experiencing the feelings of appreciation and gratitude are the flavors of sweetness and umami in life that you can taste, and it is also the life you deserve to **LIVE**.

*

Making this experience one that helps you see the world from a mysterious set of eyes, and producing a view that shows you how grateful for life you can become is of the utmost importance. During and after this adventure, you must continue to show your gratitude and appreciation for life, and share it with others. The adventure through *Systematic Desensitization* will reveal to you what could not be seen before or will help one's visual focus become more precise. Sight is extremely important because humans are visual learners. Whether you know it or not, humans learn and create a lot from sight and visualizing. For some, this may not make sense, so your challenge is to look at it from your point of view. Walk out of your front door whether it is from a box, apartment, townhome, house, mansion, penthouse apartment, hotel room, or whatever is roofing your sleeping quarters. How was the roof over your head built? Everything in the world that is built is essentially created twice. The home you live in is a home that someone created. The person that created it had a picture in their head before putting it on paper, and then to the foundation. As we start to think about creation and visualization, know an overarching goal of this book is to help you create and visualize a life where one is thriving not surviving. With visualization, you can take your mind places where it has not gone before, for wherever your mind goes, that's where you go. In order to help you see from an eagle's point of view, quickly go back and think about that ever fulfilling meal you had. When you had that meal, would it have been that great if you didn't have an awesome server or chef? Would it have been great if you didn't put that tender love and care into prepping the ingredients? Would it have been that fulfilling if you weren't in some form of discomfort, and hungry before?

Just a couple of the little things that many tend to never think about because they are such small things, yet they are also big. When you are up in a plane higher than the eagle, the world seems so small. This sheds light on how small the world really is, yet when we are on land, it seems so big. If you don't resonate with this idea, a prime example to think of is when you run into a random person at the gym, on the street, or at an outing and find out that they are friends with one of your friends. Usually people say to one another or themselves, "wow, small world". When you've been in the sky and on the land, it gives you an experience to think about. Some people really don't deeply think about their experience of flying. They are in fear of flying, worried about getting to their next destination, lost in an electronic device, reminiscing on the past rather than realizing the experience they are experiencing, or have flown so much it's just another thing. We live in such a small world that we have the opportunity to fly from one location to another in less than twenty-four hours. Do you feel people truly appreciate this? There are many people in the world who have never left their hometown. Do people really appreciate the creation of an airplane? There are about eight million people that are in the air per day, and because this is happening so often, yet not so often; the trend is that people lose that excitement of the flight. There are the select few outliers that are excited from fear, or from flying for the first time. When looking at the general population though, the excitement isn't there. When you see a child at an airport or on a plane, it is a sight to see, for they still hold and create that excitement. Something to think about is how a child's excitement is reinforced or punished while traveling. For those that have never flown, doing so can be life changing. For those that have never flown yet have seen a plane in the sky, you can see the plane looks small when it's up there. When you have the opportunity to see a plane on the ground though, it can put things into perspective. These patterns correlate to the idea that what seems to be the small moments or things in life, are also the biggest moments and things in life. This is sight looking at the big picture through the eagle's eye. For those lost on the path, and still cannot find the connection; have you ever been so hungry that you were angry (hangry), and your angriness created a chain reaction and made life even more unpleasant for you and others on top of you being hungry? These small things, parts of the journey, or moments is what makes the experience an experience. As disclosed earlier, people tend to take their experiences for granted. If you've ever been in a restaurant and the service was lacking, it most likely affected the taste of your meal. If you've ever over seasoned your food, it affected the taste of your meal. When looking at some of the moments in life, there was a moment when a server's

puppy chewed up their homework assignment for a class

they found challenging, and were near failure. That

homework assignment was chewed and due the same day

the server was serving you. This small moment in time

could have been why your server couldn't focus on serving

you at their best. This small incident to you, yet large to

them, became the deciding factor as to why you couldn't

enjoy your birthday dinner which was a large experience to

you yet at the moment seemed like a small experience to

them. For those having trouble visualizing this experience

because it's an experience you've never had, you must

understand and see that it is one that you have actually

had. This was touched on at the beginning, and if it still

doesn't make sense to you now, by the end of this

adventure, it will. For now, just note that one usually

dismisses nor thinks about what is going on with the server

rather than seeking the reason behind the lack of service because they are focused on mainly themselves. One tends to be more concerned about a meal of many meals rather than someone's education. The topic of that system will be discussed later in this adventure as well. The story of the server may not resonate with some, for that is fine. Think of that moment when you put too much seasoning onto your dish, turned a wonderful dish into an over seasoned dish, and it became a factor in which why you couldn't enjoy the product of your dinner. Again, the little things are what make the big things matter and the big wouldn't exist without the little. Expanding and diving deeper into the mind, earlier someone who was busy not enjoying their meal was doing so because of service. An aspect of this experience that needs to be addressed is that same person who is not enjoying their meal or service fails to realize the fact that they are able to afford to go out, have someone cook for them, and have someone serve them. This is an experience that back in time was only done for royalty, yet again, is an experience that people now take for granted. This in itself could be a reason why those who work extremely hard for what they've earned feel they should not have to give back to those who take life for granted, or are in some state of being in need. That feeling in itself is a causing factor of the imbalance in our world between the haves and have nots (the rich and poor), and between people and the government (secured and the ones securing). Now take these few examples and look at it with your sight. Can you see the ripple of effect? How many people do you know feel that a server giving someone a lack of service can cause chaos on a governmental and global social scale? Now you have a view of how many people see the small, and not the big. If you cannot see the ripples from the rock that has been thrown, visualize someone who is not enjoying the food that they over seasoned. While they are not enjoying their meal, they are in a state of being ungrateful. There are some out there that will be missing out on dinner when they are starving, or eating mud cakes to survive. A mud cake made from actual dirt, not that delicious chocolatey dessert that makes your mouth water. There are people who are killing their fellow human beings in order to have an over seasoned meal. This in itself could be a reason behind why there is still world hunger when there does not need to be, and why there is violence when there does not need to be. When people are blinded and cannot see, all they can do is what they know which keeps them surviving. Remember, you deserve to thrive not survive, as does everyone you are connected to. Whenever there are horses racing in constructed races on the track, the horses usually have blinders on them. The purpose of these blinders is so that the horse can run the course, or the track rather than straying away from the track that is laid out for them. If it cannot yet be acknowledged, in terms of the small picture and big picture, ask yourself if this beautiful world (the big) would exist without you (the small). If it is not realized, it must be known that the world would not exist without you. How can anything exist without your perception of it? To simplify the answer, the world cannot exist without you in it for it to exist to you. Many do not understand this fact though. This misunderstanding could be why there are many who commit suicide in the belief that the world will be the same without them, and they are not needed or wanted in it, when that is not the case at all. It is your duty to realize and know that every person you meet as well as you yourself, are extremely important. When this duty is fulfilled, you can begin to see through a larger magnifying glass, produce the sight you need in order to take care of yourself and humanity. The intention is not to be a negative nancy, so it must be known that these negative patterns are brought up in order to bring out the positive ones within you. Revealing the positive ones within you creates a ripple effect of you bringing them out of others; in turn, causing the negative patterns to diminish. Hence bringing us to the view of the present chaos in the world. With chaos comes growth. This truth brings one to wonder if the ultimate goal of humanity to find the most positive an optimal route of living is only achievable by producing mass chaos within our world. If that is the case, one wonders if there will be a period of time where there is too much chaos within our world that will lead to ultimate destruction. One wonders if we are already there. Of the many goals, one is to help alleviate the chaos in your life, that you may learn from it, and grow. You must understand that in order for you to grow, you must also help others grow. That is why we are taking this journey together, that is why the goal is to not let you falter, because not only must you grow to fulfill the purpose of humanity, you deserve to live in a state of growth rather than decay. Though you are most deserving of growth, it must be advised that you do not take your sight from the big picture, and see that not only do you deserve it; your friends, relatives, acquaintances, neighbors, and your child's friends parents also deserves it. When it comes to ultimate growth, we truly only deserve what we are willing to work for. That is why we will work together to make the journey of life the best possible for you, and your loved ones. A man/woman at the top of the mountain never wants to be there alone, as social creatures and beings, innately you will want others to be with you on the adventure of systematic desensitization. There is a saying that goes "take the path of least resistance". By going on this journey, we are taking that path, and journeying in one of the least chaotic ways one can think of. After this journey, you will have the power to help others also take the path of empowerment. Deep down, we all want to be a part of something bigger than ourselves. As humans, we've always wondered what our purpose on this rock is. This is because within all people, there is a greater intelligence that recognizes and sees our purpose, and wants to connect us to that big picture. Ask yourself if you truly know what your purpose is, or are you still trying to find it. If you don't know your answer to that question, don't be alarmed, you are not alone. After this adventure you will figure out what it is, and you will have help finding it. That is the experience and gift to be provided to you for going on this adventure.

*

Now that we've walked to the edge rabbit hole, before we hop into it, it's a duty to let you know that this hole was dug by me, as well as you, and the last bunny you saw. Being curious, and a man of the people; deciding to go deep into this hole so you would not have to was a purpose that continues to be lived out. There is also good news and bad news. Always preferring to get the bad news out of the way first, know that this hole is deep and dark. The good news, however, is that there is light at the end of the tunnel. The light is the experience, the dark is the journey; the light is you, and the dark is your shadow. You can't run from your shadow, so empower yourself in the light. In order to see the light and bask in it, the best suggestion that can be given is to read this book from the cover to the description, top to bottom, left to right, and back to front (specifically the bolded words). If you didn't start at the beginning, quickly go back and skim through. Read with a large magnifying glass rather than a small one, and with an open mind knowing that anything is possible. With an open mind, one can find that news is news; your perception and reaction to it is what makes news good or bad.

*

From living life and enduring, systematic and unsystematic forms of schooling, and learning from each and every thing; the human mind and body, are by far the most interesting things on this planet. In a world full of hazardous materials, destructive weather, and unlimited resources, humans, if you have not been able to tell, are some of the most creative and adaptable beings on our planet. The human mind and body are the centerfolds to creation and durability. This is true not only inside but also outside of the human world (society). Between the body and the mind, though not truly separate and are one, studying the mind brings the most joy. You may wonder why, and its because the mind is the most powerful resource human beings have, yet it has become the most underused tool. This map was created to empower yourself as a human being, use your mind to its fullest capabilities, as well as shed some light in hopes that it will bring to surface and out of the rabbit hole the light within you. This guide shifts between personal beliefs and experiences, common beliefs and experiences, and research along with scientific studies. On that note, if you haven't caught on yet, one of my core beliefs is that not only are we to empower ourselves, we **MUST** empower others. The words transcribed from the mind and heart are to entertain you, help you grow, find peace, be happy and spread that love. Through your evolutionary progress, enjoy the journey and the adventure!

The Calming Before The Storm

"When you are in the eye of the storm, you are often not aware of the whiplash around you"

- Hugh Bonneville

Hello fellow adventurer, the name is Chris. The process of this piece of creation started February 12, 1993. It was an early, cool morning in Yonkers, New York and Abraham Lincoln's 184th birthday. For those that can't remember that day and time of the year; from what can be remembered, it was about twenty-eight degrees Fahrenheit, snowing, and a beautiful New York day. That day is viewed as the calming before the storm. A short time after that day, an event known as The Storm of the Century had occurred. It was a category five blizzard that affected at least twenty-six U.S. States and parts of Canada. For those that don't know, blizzards are known to be the most dangerous of all winter storms. It being a category five storm means it's at its most extreme. To get a gist on how extreme this storm was; it spawned approximately eleven tornadoes, some affected areas saw five feet of snow, and the total calculated weight of snowfall was between 5.4 - 27 billion tons. Just to help you size that up; one ton is equivalent to two thousand pounds. It caused about $2 billion in damage which today is equivalent to about $3.5 trillion. This is brought up because the calm before the storm is a period of unusual tranquility or stability that seems likely to presage difficult times. *Systematic Desensitization* is correlated directly to the day I was born, February 12, 1993, and it is the calm before the storm. It is a sign or warning of what can come if changes are not made. For those that don't know, change can be made in a miniscule moment and it can be the smallest change. Become your best self, and understand the only person that can limit your powers is you. With a small change in one's life, such as knowing what you are capable of, the whole world can change. An example of this is the Butterfly Effect which is known to revolve around the idea that a flap of a butterfly's wings can cause a tornado on the other side of the world days afterwards. All that being said, the changes that need to be made can happen over night, do not need to be life altering, yet can be life changing for all present life, and future life to come. Being an African American, thinking about Ms. Rosa Parks is the perfect example. There was a split second and moment when she decided she wasn't going to move seats. After years of willingly giving up her rights as a human, that miniscule moment of change, utilizing her power of choice that she made began a revolution. Change occurs in an instant, yet also occurs over time. It is impossible for growth to occur without change. Keep in mind, when something is not in a state of growth, it is doing the opposite which is decaying, there is no in between. Think of a tree; it is on a continuous journey of transformation, and if it is not transforming, it is dead. A seed sprouts into a sapling, and becomes a tree, yet when a tree loses all its leaves, it becomes a snag. Trees are continuously evolving, and when you see evolution for what it truly is; one can admire the ultimate beauty of seeing flowers blossom, fruit growing, and colors changing. You are a tree, and the signs revealed to you are to guide you in a direction where you will not get snagged by life and rather snag life whilst taking your control over it. In a life of infinite and constant changes, it's so interesting that humans can find some changes to be so difficult. When one wonders why, it could be because people feel they do not have control over those changes. What most fail to realize is if our bodies didn't change from when we were an infant, we would not have been able to survive past childhood. You can see the failure of realization in most because once a person gets to adulthood, the tendency of change or to change is not strongly welcomed. There is a saying that goes "old people are stuck in their ways". When it comes down to it, human beings are change! Some people also believe that change is slow, it can only happen over time, and never in an instant. This mindset decelerates change. If you are one of those people, respect goes out to your thoughts and beliefs. Your challenge is to take a quick moment, think of the past minute of your existence, and ask was every second the same.

What was your answer? It's always interesting to see where one's mind goes and what the result of that question is. A second goes by extremely fast, even when you're living in the present moment. There is nothing slow about 1 second unless you're light, and if that's the case for you currently reading this; we need to have a heart to heart. For those of you who answered no to the earlier question, congrats on taking that baby step forward. For those of you who answered yes; that's perfectly fine. Expand your mind and knowledge, and you will find the guarantee that every second was not the same. Something was always different, and changing. Whether it was the words you were reading, the thoughts you were thinking, or the cells in your body; the moment was always changing in some form, shape, or fashion. That's just looking at it from a magnifying glass, or the smaller picture. Take your mind further, look out of a telescope, and see the big picture. Recognize that there is an outside world beyond your body; there is the room, street, town, city, state, country, and world you are in. The world is constantly moving, and constantly changing. Again, we are all connected, from the servers at the wedding to the bride and groom, to the person salty about their food or service.

Truly ask yourself as well as others, what changes is one making in the miniscule moments of life. Are they changes that produce a growing self and the environment they are connected to, or are they producing changes that destroy the self and that same environment?

Not to be misunderstood, the being you are, is the being you were meant to be. It is who you are that you must be in order to help the world function, and it is who you are that you must be in order to learn how to evolve yourself so that you may help others along their journey. If you have yet to understand; the being you are is different than the one you were meant to become, you must acknowledge who it is you really are in order to evolve. Regardless of who you are, ask yourself if you are the change you wish to see in our world.

To reiterate, if one is not growing or changing, they are decaying. Do you want to see a growing or decaying world? Throughout the life of a person regardless of age, status, creed, or beliefs, there is always room to grow. If there is no room or will for growth, all that awaits the individual is death. This must be acknowledged and understood because there are well over too many people that don't like looking at themselves in the mirror. These same people have an unconscious agreement with themselves until they've reached their threshold that life will always be this way for them. There are many people who are not proud of who they are or what they have become, and feel that is who they will forever be. There are people that are so unsatisfied with themselves, they feel they have the inability to satisfy others, affecting the world they live in. These are the feelings, thoughts, beliefs, and agreements that no human needs to endure, yet it is something people struggle with. Within this struggle, people go through their **OWN** lives being influenced and changed by their environment. Because people do not have the faith, or knowledge that they have influence over themselves, which in turn influences or changes their environment, people react *to* the environment rather than act *for* the environment. This chain reaction causes the effect of a decaying world. Humans are and have created a state of mind, and system of non-evolutionary change. Outside of the outliers in the world, a majority of individuals do the same thing everyday like they are a working machine reinforcing the system. They rise from their bed, get the kids ready for school, go to work, come home, eat, sleep, and repeat. Some people squeeze in a workout throughout the day whereas others don't. Bringing to fruition the fact that the United States is currently one of the most unhealthiest countries in the world. As stated earlier, when something is not growing it is decaying. When one's body is unhealthy, it is in a state of decay. Don't feel like you're being called-out specifically. Being born and raised in the States, and in this democracy, it is taught that the whole is the sum of its people. If you feel called-out, your challenge is to ask yourself why you feel that way, and dive into those feelings. What the sum of the people show, is once the work week is over, many want to live for the weekend. This is the time when people can do "what they really want to do". Some partake in activities such as going out and entertaining themselves, others take the time to rest after a long unfulfilling week, whilst some others do what their passionate about. There are seven days in the week, yet the majority of the population attempt to "live" for two - three days of the seven. Is living for the weekend truly living? If this is something that you see, why is it that it is still continued?

As history shows in the past and present day, again, not only being extremely creative, humans also have an extraordinary influence on the changes in the environment. That being said, if humans aren't consciously changing or evolving, the world may continue to be in the same state. When something is not growing or evolving, again, it is dying. With words, one can easily be misunderstood and there are a lot of words within this book, so please understand in being connected to all things, everything that we see is essentially a reflection of ourselves. This is why some feel so strongly about the problem at hand, this is what keeps some up through the night, this is also why there are over 50 million Americans on over-the-counter sleep aids. Provided the focus you put into things, the more they grow, so know the intention is not for us to focus on the problem, the intention is for us to focus on the solution. Earlier it was exclaimed that changes needed to be made or a terrible storm will arise. Maybe it's already risen, and many cannot see the whiplash it is causing. Being optimistic, it could be a category three storm right now and hasn't hit the category five stage. Think for a moment what life looks like when everyday feels the same, when everyday becomes the same, and when the world is in a collective unvarying state. A brief example of what that life is like was given earlier. Rather than it being perceived as a growing and exciting change, it may seem boring, repetitive, or even unfulfilling. This is the type of life that represents decay rather than growth. The references made are specifically in regards to the U.S. because this is where it is seen a majority of days. It is not only seen in the states though, one needs to be aware that the U.S. is one of the biggest influencers of the world. That being said, the state of decay is the current state of the planet we live on, hence why it is up to all of us to change this world of decay to one of growth. If this doesn't resonate with you wherever you are, something all of the world hears about is the 'American Dream'. What is the American Dream to you, and what does it stand for? Think on it!

Having lived on this planet, experiencing many forms of decay as you also have, the being within you is most likely extremely tired of it. This is why the blessing of you reading this is occuring. Unfortunately, there are many out there who are still unaware of the decaying days they are living, and that is exactly why it is implored that you help empower these people. In reference to the U.S.; of the many reasons why people have so much stuff going on in their lives, are always on the go, or overstimulated could be because the very reason that life can seem boring, repetitive, and unfulfilling. Living this type of life can be quite energy draining which is why people whom live in this state do not live the long lives they were meant to live, or seem dull on the day to day. People look for fulfillment and excitement in the external things we offer trying to change the moment, or make it more exciting. They look towards the external in search of the belief that the external will also re energize them. A perfect example of this is the partaking in drugs. Bare with me on this because when looking at drugs, we can bring up the illegal ones as well as the legal ones. When people look towards a drug, it gives them the belief and feeling that the drug is going to excite or dull the present moment or the experience they are having. Things such as smoking, drinking alcohol, and pill popping are extremely prevalent in this current state of decay. People resort to these external factors because they don't know how to enjoy the moment or the journey they are living. Energy levels can be low enough in individuals that they have a need to consume energy drinks or caffeine everyday in order to function. This creates the effect of addiction, and people have psychological and physiological attachments to that external source. People become drug addicts, alcoholics, acquire withdrawals when they are not digesting caffeine or sugar. The world we live in is becoming addicted to the same things that destroy their being. If this still has yet to resonate with you, another example to be thought of is how humans for so long have sought another external stimulus known as entertainment. The desire and need for these examples causes individuals to focus their sight on the external, like T.V. This focus creates the effect of individuals losing sight of themselves, again, in turn losing true sight of the world they live in. Through identifying with and desiring so much externally and with so many choices, humans have blinded themselves and weakened their ability to make the most optimal choices. Something that many people in our world partake in, is driving. Once someone has stepped into the driver's seat of a car, a person makes the choice that they will be driving. Yet while they are driving, and have the choice of doing something else, they often decide to also text whilst driving due to the psychological addiction one has to their phone. In that moment, they are essentially powerless in the choices they've made. At that same moment in time, the person is blind to the world of other drivers that they live with because of their addiction. The blinder the individual has knowingly or unknowingly put on has created the possibility or outcome of them getting into an accident. People die on an everyday basis due to car accidents, yet one wonders if they are truly accidents. There is a beauty within this scenario though. If it cannot be seen; through the choices one is making, possibilities are being created. A question that could be asked is: is the person driving the one creating these possibilities, or is it an external force that is doing the creating? When one thinks of an accident, they tend to not happen on purpose. If accidents don't happen on purpose, then it is out of the person's control. If it is out of the person's control, then it seems that person is in reality not controlling the choices or outcomes they may be creating. The desire, need, and consumption of the external has forced a system to be created to provide externally for humans. With this provision, people must understand that they are giving up their control. Not control of the world, but control of themselves. This is something many are blinded to. This system in itself actually depletes many of their being able to be which is why so many people do. This is not the first time this has been recognized by a being, yet it has yet to be recognized by the collection of humans. This is not a form of criticism, for criticism is condemning both who is being criticized, and the one criticizing. This is more a form of acknowledgment; an unveiling for those in need of help because things cannot be changed unless they are known about.

Speaking on criticism, what is most interesting about it, is humans positively reinforce it. It is another facet of the decaying state the world is in. It is believed that someone being criticized may fix, or change what is, in order to receive approval from others. Again, relying on the external in a form of social validation. With this realization, one must not blame anyone, anything, nor themselves. Positively adjusting to the awareness one acquires, an optimal route is acceptance. This is because humans do rely on the external for survival, for without the resources we have been blessed with, we would not endure. Not only is it the world that helps us to survive, it is our fellow man and woman that do the same. One must understand this in order to understand, and thrive in the world we live. The problem is the excess consumption, and dependability on the external which causes a weakness within and outside a person. This still may not have resonated with some, so I will bring up technology. We have become so strong technologically speaking that our society relies on it. If you think of the average human, and what that person goes through when they lose their phone, it is quite scary. We once lived in a world where we were concerned for our lives, the kind of food we were digesting, and if the habitat we were living in was fit for thriving; today we live in a world where people are worried how fast their internet speed is. Imagine a world where society lost power or electricity. Society would go batshit. Focusing on a solution; *Systematic Desensitization* can help expedite the process of change. Again, not to be misunderstood by the many words; looking for excitement and fulfillment in the external can be an awesome thing.

You don't bring a child to the playground, and tell them not to play. On the playground is where kids learn to run, enjoy the air they breathe, and where boys and girls learn that they have cooties. Enjoying the world we live in is strongly supported, what is being acknowledged is the imbalance.

*

Earlier it was learned that humans are visual learners. Another form of learning that helps things stick is by physical or kinesthetic touch, also known as doing or being hands on. Learning is what life for human beings has always been about, as is the playground is for kids, the world is for us. That is why being upset with the world, others, or yourself is not a suggested approach. Everyone and thing is learning. To paint a picture, think back to the days of biology when you were learning about cells. Earth has been regarded to as a living cell. We are the working organisms within it, and how it is learning to survive in the dark waters of space. Not only is Earth learning about itself through us, we are learning through it, and one another. It truly hurts you and the environment to hold any negative energy towards it or yourself. One must be compassionate towards the environment, for that is showing compassion towards oneself. It is through your uniqueness, and awareness that the world will learn about itself. In turn, if one can learn from the world they live in, they will learn about their self. An ever growing world, and expedited growth comes when you teach what it is you have learned to others. The more we help one another, the more we grow. We live in a day of time where people are extremely self-centered, so this is an important act. Reminding you that the planet or world you live in and on is a reflection of you is a reminder that in order for the world to grow, you must also grow, and vice versa. The world we live in is not perfect; in conclusion we are not perfect. Some may wonder if perfect even exists. True perfection does not exist; what is perfect is striving towards growth in every waking moment rather than decay, so do not aim for perfection, aim for progress. If the picture is yet clear for you, when we look at history, it shows humans have strived to learn about the world they live in, or the toys on the playground since day one. How is it that humans have learned about their capabilities? There is a saying that two minds are better than one, and it is within that saying that a truth comes to fruition. When it comes to consciously dabbling in the external, and communicating with the world you live in, an example to think of is traveling. It is one of the best forms of education one can have. Learning about the world one lives in by diving into different cultures, and walking on new lands can help one grow dramatically as a person. It can teach someone how to be grateful for the life they live, and also show someone how to look at things from a different perspective. Traveling is another aspect as to how humans have grown so much. If you travel to the past, you will find that humans have been, and continue to be nomadic creatures. The nomadic lifestyle of the human began to slow down when we learned that we could grow or hunt food, and find water in a specific area of land. At this moment in time is when the process of stagnation or domestication of the human being's life was most likely originated. If this thought doesn't resonate with you, take a moment to think about one of the most domesticated animals of our world. They are known as man's best friend or dogs. In the wild they're wild dogs, and wolves. They are always on the move, and always on the hunt for food and optimal shelter. When these beautiful four-legged creatures befriended man and no longer had to hunt for food or secure shelter, they became domesticated. A synonym to domestication is subjugate. Take a moment to think about the reflection that humans share with dogs, and why they are known as man's best friends. As the saying goes, you are who you surround yourself with. When looking at general society, we are looking at a cosmic magnitude of subjugation. You see this once you see how many people do not have control over themselves. Subjugation has been a part of human history for eons. The African American population knows strongly about this, yet seem to forget how long subjugation or slavery has been a part of human history. Tribes since the beginning of days enslaved foreign tribal members when battling for land. Modern day slavery is moving beyond the physical and races we've created, and towards the mental and whole of the human race. The mental in essence shifts the physical body. The subjugation of individuals is becoming a systematically conditioned process, and people are learning to naturally be domesticated within their life. Like dogs, when one is domesticated, they lose control of when they eat, go to the bathroom, and when they are able to go play on the playground. Becoming stagnant or domesticated is the opposite of what humans are truly born to do. Still yet doesn't make sense? Ask yourself how many miles a day you walk, jog, or run. It varies per culture, but the U.S. roughly moves the least, averaging under 3 miles a day. Not calling you or anyone you know out specifically; just acknowledging the truth of the whole or the reflection of you. Human's feet are made to walk well over 3 miles per day, yet in the U.S., one believes they have to put an effort into moving more than that per day. In present day, individuals have trouble moving up and down a flight of stairs. What is most interesting is even though the general population isn't physically moving, the mind is always moving creating a mindset that the individual is on the go when in fact they are not. Life is yin and yang, and a double-edged sword. The world is in a state where the balance needs to be brought back; people must stop cutting themselves, and the world we live in. Again what's being talked about, is the focus, over stimulation, and consumption the human population has and absorbs on the external. This focus has caused a loss of sight or unawareness of the internal. The blinds bestowed upon an individual causes both chaos and destruction internally, which if not remembered causes both chaos and destruction externally. The cycle continues with high numbers of individuals not being able to see or know who they are, which has been a part of the human being's purpose. People are holding swords they do not know of nor know how to wield, are cutting themselves and each other, and not fulfilling their purpose. Think of things people consume in extreme excess.

What did you come up with? Some prevalent examples that come to mind are the internet, cell phones, media, the filler activities that people deep down don't enjoy, and let's not get started on food (in regards to the U.S.). The internet and what it holds is something people rely heavily on, again, creating a weakness within individuals. Rather than going out of their comfort zone and learning, or reaching out to people; the tendency is people use the internet to find out what they want to find out. Also what is extremely common, what someone finds on the internet, is truth or fact. Whilst this book was being written in a coffee shop, the wifi collapsed, and went out. When that happened, the entire customer population within the coffee shop left, and left with negative emotions. Rather than coming together as people and conversing, most just left or got on their cellphones. Speaking of phones and cellular devices, they are constantly vibrating, ringing, beeping, and sending electrical impulses to the brain as well as body. This can cause people extreme amounts of stress, yet the trend is people feel lost or naked without their phones. Many do not even know about the electrical frequencies that travel within and around them, that their patterns of cell phone use, and the constant want or need to have them within a short distance can actually cause that addiction that was referenced earlier. One can expand their mind, and think on the term 'cellular' device. Before cell phones existed, what did cellular mean? If you don't know, again, imagine yourself back in elementary school in biology class learning what the human body is made from. Just as the earth is a living cell, the human body is made from cells. Reflection at it's finest! If you know what a device is, you will know that devices have a purpose. Do you wonder what and why your phone emits frequencies? Do you wonder what those frequencies do? Many do not, and it is because of the addiction or wanting to turn a blind eye. The addiction to these devices causes more stress in people than they can see, and because it is an addiction; it is something that people are more willing to cope with. People get that elated feeling from getting a notification or attention from that external source, and don't fret that they are in constant duress due to their device. Because you are currently reading this, you most likely fall into the spectrum of **KNOWING** rather than unknowing. Your duty is to share with others what you know, so they don't go searching the internet, finding something, and believing that they know something that they really don't. Doing so within the physical sense rather than virtual will also benefit many beings. If you don't fulfill your duty as a human, remember, you are only hurting yourself. If you have ever experienced an addiction, in the sense of you having one, you know how damaging addictions can be. If you haven't had one personally, think of someone you know that has had one, or knowing someone who knows someone that has had one. Think about the events and experiences they were having in life. Addictions can cause some major problems in an individual's life, and effect the people around them.

Just to reiterate once more on the large picture of things,

even if you yourself have not experienced something, yet

know someone who has, or know someone who knows

someone who has experienced something - including an

addiction - you are in fact connected to that; you have in

fact experienced that addiction. If you can help that person,

you are in reality helping yourself overcome that addiction.

In regards to one's purpose as a human being, to overcome

the reactions of decay and perform actions of growth

creates a wave like ripple effect. The general population

that sees only the small picture cannot realize this though,

nor can those who are in an addicted state because their

addiction is the same as the blinders that horses wear

during their races. You can see the correlation, and

understand the reasoning behind why many feel they are in

a rat race. What is the difference between a rat race, horse race, and the human race? Because you are reading this, you will acquire a perspective that puts you above the track to see how everything is moving as a whole. Have compassion and understand that certain experiences seems like one cannot live without that experience. Knowing that a person may not be able to acknowledge what seems to be a wanted desire rather than a need is a virtue that will help you spread light in other's lives. Remember that many do not know what it is they are addicted to, so it doesn't seem to them like it's happening to them or their mother; they feel it is not really affecting them. Being upset is a reason most become addicted. Being upset is what feeds the energy of the negative emotion in itself. This is why compassion is a necessary act. A part of systematic desensitization is utilizing reciprocal inhibition. Being in a state incompatible with the undesired state. When one is compassionate towards themselves and others, there is no

73

room for negative energy, and the process to eradicate an addiction can truly begin. Something that you can do as a loving, and compassionate human being is to show those who are addicted better. Be the change that you want to see. In the truest reality, you have no control over the people in the world and the environment you live in, all that it is that you hold control of is yourself. If this has yet to resonate with you, branch out, take the large magnifying glass, and see what patterns such as cell phone use has come to. Once you start to take a strong look, you can see that humans prefer to text rather than talk, and prefer to talk on the phone rather than talk in person. Look through the telescope, and outside of cellular devices. You can see we live in a world where the world is presented through a screen, and screens within screens. You have the ability to understand that watching the world from the screen sends a message to the brain that one is experiencing what they see on the screen. Because they've had that virtual experience, one feels they do not need to go out physically to see it or experience it themselves. Do you feel people wonder where the creation of VR (virtual reality) is derived from? Do you know that it is a creation of present day, but the thought has existed for centuries? Outside of the cell phone use, media, and internet, we live in a world where people have a plethora of "filler" activities that they don't truly enjoy, but use to fill up their day because they need these experiences to feel like they are actually living. These activities fulfill the day rather than fulfill the person. A great example of this are jobs. A job is meant to make a living, yet now it is a person's living. People live to work, and do not work to live. For example, the copious 9-5 jobs people work, yet say they hate, or just go through the motions of daily in order to pay the bills they don't want to pay. This is synonymous to how people eat (in the U.S.):

people live to eat, rather than eat to live. People now look and feel a certain way they don't want to look or feel, yet are not willing to diet or workout. Again, not to be misunderstood; the fact that one can find something on the internet without having to go on an extreme journey, minimize one's energy expended to acquire knowledge is awesome. The fact that mom, dad, or your lover can be called from many miles away, and not have to wait weeks for a letter or hours for travel to talk with him or her is wonderful. The fact that someone wanted to create such visual forms of entertainment in order for everyone to see parts of the world they haven't seen, expand one's thoughts and creativity, and give people the chance to netflix and chill after an eventful day is a blessing. The fact that we have so many opportunities in the states for people to acquire a means to live is inspiring. All that being said, it is about balance. People utilize all the gifts they have in excess, without true appreciation, and it causes people to take things for granted. People consume so much, and do so blindly. They do not know what it is they truly consume, nor how it affects them. The overstimulation and consumption through the systems we have created is causing an extreme disconnect not only between people and their environment, also between people and themselves. I speak of all these things from the perspective of living in the United States, I speak of all these things in knowing how influential the United States is to the rest of the world. With no experienced knowledge of the world someone lives in or themselves, a person will look for those experiences and knowledge from Google. Instead of physically traveling, communicating, or catching up with a friend that they haven't seen or talked to in years, they will text, or talk on facebook. Instead of leaving the house and seeing what's really going on in the world, people watch and read the news. After working eight or more hours in the day for someone else's dreams, a person will sit on the couch, eat fast food, watch netflix, and forget about their dreams. Because people are so concerned with the little things in their life that keep them busy and disconnected from the world they live in, like the effects a bad grade on a test can have on someone. People lose concern about the big things such as poverty stricken families around the world that can't send their child to school to even take a test. People are more worried about their internet moving slow than famine in a 3rd world country. People are concerned more with how they look rather than connected to how they feel. Due to this extreme loss of connection, there is a deep to superficial and superficial to deep chain reaction that is caused. People are disconnected to themselves causing them to become disconnected to their purpose. Not being connected to one's purpose gives one a sense of unfulfillment, which then causes people to destroy rather than construct. For those that see and try their best to focus on the beauty; pessimism is not the intent. We live in a beautiful world of creation and life, but the truth is, we are destroying faster than we are creating. Not only that, the general population is growing rapidly, and it is growing most rapidly in the places of decay rather than growth. The connection people have to themselves, and the connection they have to their environment are the largest changes that need to be made. With this purpose and drive in mind to help produce a growing world, we will see a dramatic difference in our relationships between ourselves and the environment. This can happen with the smallest of changes in one's behavior. Again, we are all connected and all affect one another. Your change becomes someone else's change, and this is how the butterfly effect works.

*

A **KEY** to happiness is not only to find those consistent and empowering changes that help you live a more fulfilling and connected life. True happiness will come when you help others do the same. Admittingly, some changes are an acquired change, just as some tastes are an acquired taste. Change can easily occur when one believes that doing something sometimes causes discomfort in the short game, yet helps one become what they need to become in order to thrive in the long game. It's been said before that growing through your discomfort only makes you stronger. This idea is reinforced with an activity such as working out. Getting out of bed, or going after work to get a workout in can be a challenge at times. Yet once you get to your area of growth, it's all downhill. Once one begins to push themselves, test their limits, and reach new thresholds, they learn that working out is extremely beneficial for them. After achieving a period of growth, releasing endorphins, and accomplishing something, working out gives a person a sense of fulfillment, and the ripple effect continues. The person sees massive improvements in life; physically, they are in the best shape they've ever been in. Because they are taking care of their body, they begin to take care of their environment. Next thing you know their environment starts taking care of them, they are respected by society for their dedication and hard work, desired by others, complimented by others boosting self esteem, and so on. When one works through that discomfort that leads to growth, they become stronger, more lively, and focused. Working out is one illustration of an empowering change that changes life for the better rather than the opposite. Being a millenial, it has been bestowed upon us to grow up in an ever changing world. Having seen our society grow in drastic measures such as creating technologies that many could only have dreamed of, finding medicines that can cure a multitude of diseases, building cars that don't need a human to function, and forming an intelligence that is not organic yet can function almost like the human mind has been a blessing and a curse. Though there are many beautiful minds out there still creating as well as turning dreams into reality; the overstimulation we have produced for our minds has the general population reaching what seems like a plateau of human existence, and living in a constant dream state. This dream state is the same one in which the attentive focus to escape reality causes one to lose sense of reality, creating an illusion. We can expedite the progressive changes we have seen in our world as well as in ourselves in hopes that we can progress towards a world of growth, creation, and movement rather than decay, plateauing, and stagnation. This is why this book was created. The beautiful world seen from an eagle's eye can be one where people have faith and dependability in themselves, and not in external objects. It is one where people are living freely in peace, happiness, and growing. This world is the same world where hope is gained, not lost, or forgotten. This is the big picture, this is what we can make a reality. There are others that understand and want to see this, and that is who we are working with. There are those out there that are tired of all the decaying acts we've self produced, and willing to lose sleep in order to produce growth. Though this is the world some of us see, the change must be a collective one in order to be truly effective. This is important, for one person can change the environment, yet at the same time, one's environment can change a person. While reading this map, and focusing on the solution together; we will find in this adventure an awakening of and putting gas towards our inner flame, so that we may stay warm and have light during the New

Age, Storm of the Century. It must also be remembered

after a storm comes a rainbow, and after a storm the sun

shines.

Freeing Yourself From The System

"To know, is to know you know nothing at all.

That is the meaning of true knowledge"

- Socrates

Since the beginning of time of what can be remembered; **A QUESTION** of life is why people do the things they do, and why they think the way they do. Take a quick second and grab a pen, or pencil. If you were asked this question, write down what your answer would be.

Below the answer you just wrote, write down *your* life question. If you cannot think of it off the bat, no worries, welcome to the human mind. If you can, congratulations on being ahead of the game. Once you've taken the time to find some answers, and come up with another question, what other questions has the answers led you to if any? Will you implement what you find into your life? Once you can continue to ask questions and even question the answers, life becomes more adventurous, and fulfilling. If you cannot answer your life question or don't know it, yet have continued to read on, that is perfectly fine, you are not alone. To find

your life question, a suggestion is to remember what it was that you were most curious about as a child. What was it that you **HAD** to know?

If you can't remember back that far, do your best to look into each and every action you take today or tomorrow, and ask yourself, why **YOU** are doing it. Things will come to light at these moments in time, and you may learn more about yourself than you possibly have ever known. How to find the answer to your life question is to hold onto that written question, if it is written. Read it everyday, and keep it at the forefront of your mind. Studies have shown that writing things down on paper perpetuates it into reality like magic and spell books, so begin creating your spell book. Holding that question with you on a daily basis and asking that question every moment you get will lead you to answers. Question those answers, and that will get you closer to the truest answer of your life question which is the ultimate truth. If you can do this wholefully and faithfully, it will lead you to live a quest of passion and curiosity which will ultimately lead you to fulfillment. You can then begin to live a life with a mind and body that isn't imprisoned in an illusion, and live in a beautiful reality. Something realized these past couple of decades is humans have not been asking many questions of late. With the internet, phones, and the resources we have on hand, it makes people feel as if we don't know something, we can know something instantly so we do know something, when in truth, we know nothing. As is everything in life, the access is a useful and deadly tool. It has been noticed that if something entertains a person, makes them feel good for a short period of time, if a person with a title or an organization says something, people tend to absorb and believe whatever is said, and accept it as the ultimate truth. That is until that truth turns out to seem or be untrue, and then a person will question their beliefs that may have been held and reinforced for who knows how long. The ripple effect that rises from this is because the person does not know what to believe, they will begin to absorb a plethora of similar beliefs to their old way of thinking in order to validate how it was they thought. The cycle continues, and continues creating a person who doesn't know themselves. Humans also tend to not question the answers they receive if they feel they can't truly comprehended the answer; fearful of owning up to ignorance. In these cases, it is common that a smile, a head nod, and acceptance occurs. This creates the reinforcement of false beliefs that in turn will grow and spread. At times, an answer can be something a person wants to run away from, or don't want to hear because they're in a state of denial or fear. In other instances, an answer can oppose someone's beliefs or way of life, hence they don't question their current belief or life that they've worked so hard to grow and protect. Because of fear and the ego, people are quick to turn a blind eye or not question what is said or believed, and accept almost anything as an answer or truth. If this concept has yet to resonate with you, do you believe everything that was just stated? If yes, why? If not, how can you not? This is where people become imprisoned within their minds, and where a problem lies. An example of this is the telecommunications Sprint commercial (keep in mind, watching or listening to commercials is not a suggested activity to indulge in). The commercial is of Thomas Middleditch, who is well known for his role in the awesome television series Silicon Valley. Thomas asks the question: *how* much would you pay for something you don'twant? This is so creative, and extremely humorous. What would you answer? The best guess is $0, yet many have a $1,000 device that they hate getting notifications from because of the stress it can cause and are imprisoned by it. Many have thousands of dollars invested into a degree or piece of paper they don't use. Further illustrating acceptance, a prime representation are the foods that people eat. How often do you believe people read their nutrition labels/packages, or truly wonder about them? Some studies suggest that about 70% of Americans don't utilize the nutrition facts on their food labels. It has also been revealed what is on the ingredients of some labels of food, and even medicine is not in fact truly present in what one is ingesting. Some ingredients in foods or supplements have even been linked to certain diseases and cancers, yet people still ingest them. People are imprisoned due to their ignorance, and fear of owning up to it. As long as it's on the shelves, it must be okay to eat is the mindset of much of America. This mindset in itself has generated a pandemic of obesity and other lifestyle diseases. It has gotten to a point where there is a great lack of self-control or acknowledgement of thyself, and lives are again not being controlled by one's self. Topics like this are scary; it's something one would want to run from. Maybe even you want to run from it, yet we both prefer to know and seek the truth, so we don't turn a blind eye. It can't be said for everyone out there that they are seeking the truth. The saying ignorance is bliss holds true in this regard. With you currently reading this book, it is something you may wonder about, and have also acknowledged rather than ignored. Playing devil's advocate, it's understandable coming from the point of view that when we come into this world, what do we know as babies? We are raised based off of the knowledge and beliefs of our parents, teachers, and peers. The real question is not what do we know as babies, it is, what do they know? Our parents were taught by their parents, teachers, and peers and teach to us what worked for them during their time. If recalled again, this is how humans have grown and learned; there is a point when things need to be taken with a grain of salt though. As millennials may know, the times today are a lot different than the time of their parents and ancestors. The light is not to be shined on just generation Y. This is a true fact of all generations; the light is especially bright for millennials because of the amount of changes made within their generation. Another question to ask is outside of parents and peers, who are our teachers taught by? These are the people that are paid to teach our society - an extremely important job! Other than the same group our parents were taught by, to my knowledge, in order to teach at a public school, which is funded by the state, one must have a degree to teach. This degree is acquired through a process of learning what and how to teach by someone other than the teacher. It's understandable for one can only teach if one learns. Once we begin to broaden our horizons, we find a teacher in a public school is not teaching what they want to teach, they are following and teaching a certain curriculum, and teaching what they are told to teach. Some of the rebel teachers which are necessary teach outside the curriculum, and all teachers have their own teaching style within the curriculum. This brings to fruition the fact that what we learn as students is not ultimate truth, for it is altered based off of institutionalized demand. The information is not only taught from the teachers perspective, but also learned from a students perception. Each student hears, and looks at the teacher differently. Outside of the perceptions of the student, the one who is learning, and the teacher, the one who is teaching, the curriculum is in fact created by another. The prevalence and importance of this matter comes to focus when thinking on the elementary years. This is when our brains are absorbing the most, while it's not able to comprehend everything we are learning. At a young age, children are being overstimulated with different forms of knowledge and reinforced based off their ability to accept what is being taught. To make a long story short, a majority of kids are being taught what the school system wants them to learn, not what they need to learn or want to learn. In this system where children spend most of their time, they are taught who they "should" be, and positively reinforced for accepting what they're told rather than questioning. What's really troubling is once a child grows up, due to the conditioning, reinforcement, and punishment, young teens go thousands of dollars into debt by reason of feeling that's what they *should* be doing. They then become a indebted and/or mechanical human being partaking in a life in which they feel they have no choice, and must pursue life from a perspective shaped by society or the system. Teachers not teaching what they want to teach, and more of them teaching what they are told to teach could be why many kids go through their days not enjoying school, or why adults don't enjoy their career. This brings to mind an early morning when pre-grade school kids were walking to their bus stop. The look on these kids faces was not a look of excitement, joy, or wonder. They didn't seem happy about having the chance and opportunity to go out, experience life, and learn something new. While having a conversation with a mother, she pointed out that her high school child didn't have much motivation to be active or care about school, and this was something that she saw in many teenagers in present day. A different mother who is a full time mom wants to raise her boys to be great people, yet with the excess stimulation in their environment and school, she finds it challenging to raise her boys to be fully aware of the world they live in. What does this say about the schools that we create? What does this say if it begins at such a young age? A majority of kids do not appreciate life, nor the blessings that they receive. These same children will not be happy when they wake up, nor will they realize the significance of waking up to a new day. They aren't grateful that they are able to get a ride to school and don't have to walk ten miles to get to school, and walk ten more on the way back. Many are not grateful that they receive an education, when there are those who don't. Many kids are ignorant to these blessings, and that same ignorance is reinforced. This continues to late adulthood, and is a part of the educational system, or how humans learn from a young age. We are all connected and share these experiences. It is mainly whether you can learn and understand how to use this knowledge within your life. Earlier it was asked, what do human beings know as babies coming into this world. A theory that comes to mind is that babies of the universe hold and know all the secrets, and knowledge of life. As a baby coming out of the womb, we are not able to communicate this knowledge verbally, nor act on it with undeveloped bodies. An objective of life is to tap into one's deeper self and retrieve the secrets, and knowledge that we've always held. In present day, most babies come into this world tainted and overstimulated as soon as they come out the womb, and begin to slowly forget all these secrets. Similar to how adults are slowly forgetting about themselves. At the beginning of life, we are so vulnerable that in order to survive, we must stay close to those who birthed us or guard our livelihood. This is how a systematic process of conditioning and learning begins. In order to survive, those older than the ones needing to be taken care of teach how it is that they have survived. If what is taught is not adhered to, one is punished or negatively reinforced. If what's taught is accepted, one is rewarded or positively reinforced. Some become so accustomed to this way of life that a characteristic called learned helplessness can arise. It is a condition of one feeling powerless due to their lack of being able to succeed or do anything correct. This condition is thought to be a causing symptom of depression. How interesting that is with depression being one of the leading psychological illnesses today. Hope is not lost! Once we acquire the knowledge of our guardians, and begin to formulate our own autonomy, one can tap into their innate knowledge of the universe. This can take years to come to, which is why I'm grateful I could create this map. Interestingly enough, in order for this process to truly occur, we must become vulnerable again. Vulnerability is a necessary part of growth. People tend to use the word, and automatically get defensive when they must be it. When one is vulnerable, they are opening themselves up. One must be open in order to receive. When being vulnerable, know that you are not only always a student, you are also always a teacher. There will be times when you must continue to learn, and times when you must teach. There is an awesome saying that goes "one should teach what it is they're trying to learn". Think for a moment! Even as a baby who is extremely vulnerable, and relies on others to live; those who the baby relies on also rely on the baby. If the caretakers of children did not have children, how could they learn to grow and be a caretaker. If one cannot take care of a small child, how can one take care of a bigger child (themselves)? The baby is truly

vulnerable, yet if the parent doesn't do the same, they will

not be able to raise the baby in the most optimal fashion.

The tendency of becoming a parent is no easy task. In

reality, we are parenting ourselves our whole life, hence

learning our whole life how to live the best life. If one isn't

open to learning, they can never learn. There is this funny

thing called the ego that usually gets in the way of humans

performing the correct role at the correct moment. The ego

is known as a person's self esteem or sense of self-

importance. It is that hidden voice within your mind in

which people identify strongly with. In psychology, the

ego is known as the voice in your head that always says I,

me, or my; it is the bridge between consciousness, and

unconsciousness. The ego uses fear as it's ally, and feeling

fear is what humans fear most. Though we don't like the

thought of feeling fear or being fearful, we can be quite

comfortable in this state. Ego will use fear as a lifelong resort if you let it. It's a challenging cycle to break, and a resort one may never want to leave. It is quite common for people to be in a state of fear, because when in a state of fear, all of a person's actions and reactions are "meant" to keep them safe and secure. This could be why everyone feels their actions and reactions are okay, or what validates them. If it doesn't make sense to you, we will go deep into this. Think of that one friend who hates their job, yet because of the fear of not paying their bills, or what will happen if they leave, they stay at their job. Take a moment to wonder if you ever held the experience of raising your hand in class when you didn't understand something, or were you fearful of looking dumb in front of the class so you didn't raise your hand. Maybe you've heard your teacher say something that you knew for a fact was false, yet didn't call the teacher out because of the fear of repercussions. Maybe it has never been your teacher, but instead your friends. You knew what they were doing may just not be the smartest thing, yet didn't voice your concern. It is common within friends, family, or significant relationships to have the fear of being outcasted from the homies, significant other, mom and dad, or boss, so nothing is said. All due to fear, ego, and avoiding that fear because one is afraid of feeling that fear due to their ego. As a baby coming out of the womb and into a new world, there is a continuous duality of unconscious and conscious fear of the unknown. There is an inevitable ignorance and innate curiosity that human beings have held since first becoming self-aware creatures, and that is shown when we come out the womb. Those who care for the babies also have the power to nurture the babies based off of their knowledge, and hold a power they have yet to know. With no knowledge of the unknown, innate curiosity, and the desire for humans to control what they feel they know, a series of unfortunate events forms. The sum of fear and the ego have produced what is now known as the fear of missing out (FOMO). FOMO is a newly recognized mental disorder, and has been prevalent throughout human history, yet is seeming to become a destructive pandemic due to social media, and technology. It must be known that this fear is not something you are not born with. It is a fear instilled into a person by society because of its own fears and doubts which has been passed down through families and expanded through communities with time. Keep in mind: society is you, everyone you know, and everyone you don't know. Yes, parents, older siblings, grandparents, uncles, aunts, and teachers all pass it down to the children of the world. Again, do not blame them, for a lot of them never intended to do so. A lot of family, friends, and loved ones just want the best for you. There is that famous saying in the Bible that Jesus says while he's being crucified. It goes something like, "Lord, forgive them for they know not what they do". Think on it for a moment; have you ever felt anxious because you felt you were making the wrong decision, missing out on certain activities or events, not knowing what is going on in your world, or not being able to connect with others? This feeling or list of feelings is something that just about everyone at one point or another in their life feels. These are the symptoms of FOMO and just like the flu, it can easily be passed around. When a person is in a state of fear, they can project that fear unto others, then others become afraid, project their fear, and the process continues. An example of how this can be easily passed down is if something hurt or damaged a parent. The parent desires so strongly to protect their child from the pain they felt, they unknowingly or knowingly instill that fear into you, and try to unwrite it from your life as well. A troubling aspect of FOMO is when it is brought up; it is sometimes thought of as a joking matter, and laughed about. This is why it must be known for what it is, how it can be passed down, and how contagious it can actually be. This may be the most detrimental mental disorder to our society. Yes, more damaging than one of the leading mental disorders in the U.S. known as depression that can cause people to go as far as to take their own life. This is something if not addressed, the world as we know it, the people you know and love, maybe even yourself will no longer have control over their minds or actions AKA their life. The world will and may already be, controlled by fear. When those in fear see those not in fear, they will be the sheep that want to be protected by the shepherds. If you cannot comprehend the power that fear has, how do you think Hitler got a whole country to back him, and kill millions of innocent people? He capitalized on the country people's fear. If one uses their ability to not fear, let their ego not get the best of them, and not let the system control them; they will have the freedom to live. To live is not the same as being alive, and singer/rapper Drake said it himself, "everybody dies but not everybody lives". These two sayings reveal a secret that a lot of people overlook. What everyone should know is a system does not work without it's parts, and we don't know what we don't know. If you feel like you've been imprisoned, or are in a place that you don't want to be in; know that you can free yourself, know you are not stuck, know that you are in control. Once you reach this point in your life, you can begin to recognize the 'being' aspect of your human being. Once you are able to connect with this side of your humanity, the world is a different place; life is a different thing. Its as if you died, and came back to life. Once you come to this moment you decide whether you want to be a sheep or a shepherd. Throughout time, our self awareness has created a sense of control. Because we are aware, we have the ability to control our thoughts and our actions. There is a saying though, use it or lose it. If one doesn't use their thoughts or act rather than react, they lose those abilities.

*

Earlier, life questions were discussed, and you were asked to find and answer yours. A core belief is we all have a life question. We have this question because there is something deep within us that we know, yet can't remember. It is something we want to remember and know. Again we have our egos, and fears that can easily slow us down or keep us from finding and remembering what we truly desire. Not only do fear and ego slow us down, the system we live in does the same. The ego, fear, and the system, all of which are powerful influencing forces are only powerful because one gives them power. They are forces that we can all overcome. With that being said, it takes the inner flame within *you* and the will to unleash it in order for you to be free. Finding the answer to your life question, remembering what it is that is deep within you, and applying the memoirs that come to light to the world in which you were born correlates to what one could deem as one's life purpose. When one can achieve these obstacles that we as well as others put out for ourselves, life becomes as fulfilling as it was always meant to be rather than being unfulfilling, chaotic, and decaying. Whether one is consciously aware of their question or not, this question, and this innate desire is what directs the path they walk in life. From asking the couplet of a single question, why humans do and think the way they do, and it leading to answers and more questions; it has produced what some would call a beautiful life or a dream. Admittingly, it wasn't always beautiful from a certain point of view nor will it always feel that way; yet those uncertainties make it that much more beautiful. The imperfection that we see and find in life can always be changed to get us one step closer towards wholeness, or connection to the perfection that we seek. In the truest reality, again, there is no such thing as perfection, which is why you will always be in a constant state of growth. If one can see the silver lining in what it is that you yourself and others have created towards that wholeness, the only word that comes to mind is wowzers. Throughout the journey of learning and understanding others, we make life so much harder than it needs to be. It's so funny that we do this because humans throughout history have searched to find ways to make life as easy as possible. The belief is we do this because we like challenges. Regardless of how small or large something is that you've set out to achieve, when a challenge is overcome, or an objective completed; it gives you a feeling and sense of achievement as well as accomplishment. This euphoric feeling releases chemicals in the brain that naturally make people happy and confident. Think of your past, the challenges you overcame and the objectives you've completed. How did they make you feel? What if the challenge was bigger, harder, more extreme? Would it make your sense of happiness more extreme? Do you have a current challenge or objective that you've placed on yourself in order to achieve a goal, or do something you've never done? Are you trying to graduate school, acquire a promotion, starting your own business, changing your health practice, learning something new? This is how humans have grown to be such creative, strong, and resilient beings. Complete your challenges and achieve through expressing your truest self, and do it in the most creative way you know possible. There are many out there who feel they are not creative whatsoever, yet they themselves are one of the most creative creations this universe has to offer. Recently over a couple of games of pick-up basketball, there was the chance to catch up with an old peer. It was disclosed to him that this book was being written, and this old friend said, "I don't know how authors do it". He wanted to one day write fiction, yet didn't truly feel he could. This is for him, and everyone out there that needs to know, you are creativity!! When you can realize that, your creative bone will grow strong and unbreakable. Always remember the only person that is strong enough to keep you from doing anything you desire is yourself. Always remember resilience will move you forward in life, and help you find the answers that you seek. Always remember your life question, and ,continue to question the answers you receive. The answer to the life questions asked earlier is: people do what they do in order to survive in the environment they are born into; people think the way they do because their environment creates a system, also known as a belief system. When this is realized, the system and the environment that we live in will be questioned.

The System

"The meaning of life is that it is to be lived, and it is not to be traded and conceptualized and squeezed into a pattern of systems"

- Bruce Lee

Previously discussed was the power of the ego, and it's relationship with fear and the system. Ego has grown and endured because of the roles **WE** have created as humans. If we look back to the beginning days of human culture, they revolved around tribes. Within one's tribe, they **ARE** given or born to fit a specific role. This is still true, and is very applicable to present day families. The problem truly escalated when people started to not fit into the roles they were positioned to be in. Once that occurred, people did not know where they fit in at all, and this created a lost human being. A lost soul is one that will take dramatic measures to be found. When one is lost, they feel alone, afraid, and outcasted from the collective. These characteristics transform a person to be willing to do whatever is necessary in order to gain appreciation, attraction, acceptance, or love. This could be a reason behind the increased number of shootings in the U.S. within the past decade. The states of fear produced from the stray soul feed not only the ego, but let others capitalize on that fear. In order to gain the feeling of belonging, and avoid the fear of being outcasted, people search for connections through many external sources. When thinking about where people find the feeling of belonging to a tribe, where do you think people find this feeling?

Already discussed was the religious system which formulates its separate tribes of denominations, and the governmental system which formulates its tribes through political parties. Through what else do people seek to create and form egotistical and fear based connections? We could bring up sports, music, drugs, TV & entertainment, gyms, workplaces, and network events. It can be seen nearly everywhere, which shows the spider web we live in. The school system reinforces the ritual of roles, and the prevalence can be seen especially in high school. This is when kids formulate their own tribes within the school, for example, you have the jocks, the emo kids, punks, nerds, geeks, etc. What happens to those that don't find the tribal energy they hope to become apart of? Those are the kids that tend to resort to violence and drugs. The system we live in positively reinforces the growth of these tribes, and it is because of the capital and power gained. When we look at the human population, and the life questions that every person has, one could wonder if you have thought about the collective life question of the human being race rather than the separated people and the tribes they belong to. Some would say it is: what are human beings on this planet to do? This collective curiosity has definitely killed the cat, and forced the collective to take catastrophic measures. Within the human system, humans have become so curious, wanting to find answers, and bring about growth from performing roles; they are willing to suffer themselves, and kill and destroy other living beings including other humans. When it comes down to it, all humans have been lost since day one, and are still on this lost path today. From an analytical perspective, it makes sense to have roles within a society, so that the society can operate optimally. Unsystematically speaking, one wonders in a world of no roles, what does everyone become? **EQUAL!!** In a world full of roles, what then occurs? Systems are created, and separate organizations such as tribes manifest. Roles in themselves are illusions that were created by people in order to give them a feel and sense of purpose that feeds the ego. Roles make humans feel as if they are doing what they are "supposed to be doing" on this planet rather than just living. When looking deeply into it, are the roles being assigned by someone other than the person trying to fill that roll, or is the role of someone created by others and a person is conditioned to fit that role?

For those that don't understand the system, let's learn more about the system, and break it down. On the grand scale, we are habitants of a universe. The universe is something that is out of our control; it includes the stars, galaxies, and other planets. Something we are all a part of, yet something we don't know too much about. With that being said, once you reach a certain point in life, you have the power to understand the universe as if it were your backyard, or you were one with it. Within the universe, there is a galaxy we have termed the Milky Way, within the Milky Way is a Solar System, which is where the planet Earth resides. The Solar System is the sun and the planets that revolve around it. When looking at planet Earth, it is an ecosystem. As we can see, the word system keeps generating, illustrating why we are living in a system. As we break down the larger picture or the larger system, the most outer layer of our planet is the atmosphere. This is where the sky and clouds are. On the outer edges of our atmosphere, we have planets and stars. You then have the biosphere which is where you'll find us; an organism of this large ecosystem. The land we walk on is a part of the geosphere, and the waters we swim in are a part of the hydrosphere. The Earth would not be able to sustain our lives without these working parts. They produce oxygen for us to breathe, water for us to drink, lands for us to grow crops and live on. Within the ecosystem we live in, there is another system. It seems similar to the natural ecosystem, yet is not. This system is one created by man, not one of the natural universe. In the truest reality it must be known that it is natural, and one of the universe. The mind may have just got boggled there. To put it simply, it is in truth natural because we are a product of the universe as the universe is a product of us. One may wonder how the human system is similar to that of the universal system? Do we not have grocery stores that produce food and water for us, a housing system that provides shelter for us, air ventilation systems to produce cold, hot and clean air, and so on. The real question is who is in control of these systems? The **WORKING PARTS** of this system are humans that use the most powerful tool we have, the mind, in an attempt to control as much of the system as they can, which in turn controls those with less control of their minds. Our own self is what we can control, there is nothing else. Because of this desire for control, the system humans have created is malfunctioning and destroying the larger system. The planet is in a decaying state, because humans are not controlling themselves, and trying to control what is out of their control. The movie "Spiderman" recognized and let us know with great power, comes great responsibility. For some reason or another, human beings don't like to be responsible. It could be the ignorance is bliss factor. In the sense that because, one doesn't know, they don't need to be responsible. The underlying secret is that everyone does know, so if they are not taking responsibility, they are okay with the world dying and are contributing to it. When thinking about the human system, because the system is so chaotic, it is in fact truly uncontrollable. This is why when humans reach for power, they always want more and never have enough. When discussing the system we live in, we've touched base on the school system, but it must be known that what keeps the system going is our governments, religions, and corporations. For now, to keep it simple, we will discuss more about the schooling system, and it's part in the conditioning process. For those who do not know what conditioning is, in layman's, it is when something or someone is being altered or trained to be a certain way. The schooling system is something that a majority of the U.S. population goes through. People are put into classrooms which in reality is confinement in a big box.I remember telling my mom in my early days of school that I was essentially in a prison with books. Think about it for a second: when in school, children are told how to act, when to act, and what to believe. The schooling system is where people are made to be something they are not, and more of something others want them to be. When a person doesn't conform to the norm of acting how they "should", or acting out, they are ridiculed and punished. For those of you that didn't catch that, when you *act out*, you are not acting "in" the norm. Does this remind you of society, your family, or how your tribe functions? Remember earlier how it was discussed how often this process takes place, how easily it can be passed down and around, how it can spread like cancer. When we look at most schools, think about what are they feeding children. At peak times of growth, do kids need to be indulging in pizza, fries, and fried chicken to create the most optimal functioning human being? This could be the reason why in present day USA, most adults crave pizza, fries, and fried food. Due to budget cuts, or whatever it may be, recess time or P.E. is diminishing and is sometimes not even required for students. This could be the reason why in present day USA, most adults are not physically active. The combination of food cravings and inactivity, though a "highly developed" country, the U.S.

is one of the most unhealthiest and obese countries in the world. In the schooling system, due to the structured curriculum, creativity is frowned upon. Rather than developing creativity and intellect, the schooling system is teaching people how to work or become machines, rather than how to create work or machines. See what is in the process of being created!? Another system that teens and adults partake in on a daily, yet may not really recognize, is the driving or road system. People are conditioned from a young age to have hopes and aspirations as young children to stop walking or riding on the school bus, to get their license, and drive. Have you ever wondered why the roads are built where they are, and what they are leading or directing you to? The roads driven and walked on are specifically designed to take us to certain designed locations. There are signs and lights that demand attention, tell people when to go or stop, where and where not to turn. At a glance, schools and the roads seem logical for a majority of people because this is what they grow into. One must recognize that if they don't follow the signs, go to school, or follow the "rules", they are punished or negatively reinforced for not following what is "supposed" to be the norm. If you are not living life by systematic design, you are told and treated as if you are not living "the proper" life. When following the rules, you are in fact being ruled. There is an old saying to instill fear into others that goes "the banana that gets away from the bunch always gets peeled". With an eagle's eye view, it looks like another way to direct people within their lives. It seems like a way to condition you to live a life designed *for* you, not *by* you; again, an old tribal ritual. A reason why in the truest sense, no one can control humans is we have this superpower called free will. If we choose to disobey law, not convert to a religion, disobey teachers, or run through traffic lights, we will and do. Some people recognize the system we live in, and others don't; that's why this map was created. Those who aren't aware of the system are usually the ones being controlled by the system. When saying controlled, it is in reference to one losing self-awareness and thought, which in turn has one lose control of their actions and environment. Again, one cannot control their environment, all it is that they can control is themselves. Still, one must understand that the environment is a reflection of their self. Once one loses control, they are conditioned to follow the group norm because they don't know who they are, or what their purpose in life is. When that happens, because of fear, the ego, and the systems reinforcement, a person will do what everyone else is doing because it's "normal". It's a route that is less of a challenge, and one feels more connected to the world because they are doing everything the world is doing or what they are being told to do. When one has this feeling, they feel they will be rewarded by society, for that is the conditioned feeling they are taught to have. This feeling could be where the term peer pressure arose from. You know that feeling of your gut telling you don't want to do something yet your friends are doing it, and if you don't do it they criticize you or if you do do it they praise you. Haha, I said do do... Humans are social creatures, so peer pressure is something that can easily drive them to do things they truly don't want to do, yet may drive them to actually want to do something. The system uses this innate human need of connection and social status. Recently having had the blessing of speaking with an acquaintance who just purchased a new Mercedes Benz, he was most passionate about not the vehicle in itself, but the membership he acquired with the vehicle purchase. Because he has a Benz, he is able to park in specific locations marked specifically for Mercedes at the Mercedes Benz stadium in Atlanta. He gets free car details, discounts on services, and etc. With Mercedes Benz being a luxury car, what it represents is one is living a luxury life. This is social status at it's finest, and the benefits with the Mercedes membership positively reinforce this belief. The corporation of Mercedes knows this, and leads people to spend copious amounts of their energy and life span in order to gain access to that feeling. This is how they capitalize themselves within the system.

One of the most mind-controlling aspects we have in present day is media and cell phones. Think about the news, and the things that are projected to instill fear into others, or make them believe something from a few snippets of videos that don't tell the whole story. Think about social media, and that feeling of connection because someone liked a photo or post. It is the same thing as media, it is just society partaking in the propaganda. We are helping prolong and empower this system. Having the chance to speak to an old friend from high school, we were discussing how our 10 year reunion is coming up. Because of social media, we already know what everyone is doing, what jobs they work, how many kids they've had, etc. From a certain point of view, people are slowly losing the ability to have real life connection with individuals, and instead relying on virtual connections. With humans focusing on the virtual side, people don't have the chance, or ability to grasp genuine human connection. The connection created by media is an illusion that feels real because one clicked a button. This illusion that is seen in one, the whole population can start to become. There are plenty of people who post things on social media who appear one way, and they are a completely different in person. Again, when one is engrossed in the illusion, they cannot grasp the whole story or see the bigger picture. Have you ever said or thought while watching a movie, TV show, skit, or music show that it would be cool to meet a famous person in real life? Did you catch that?Does the life you are living seem like a real one? The same people controlled by the system usually feel as if they have no choice in the actions they take, or take actions without truly thinking about the repercussions. They are in constant fear, self-doubt, and have a burning desire to be a part of the norm.

*

What is it you fear? What is it you doubt? What is it you have a burning desire to be a part of? These are questions that a more complex part of our system has capitalized on. In the beginning, God created the heavens and the earth. This is something that many of us have heard throughout our lives. For those who haven't, it is the first sentence in the Bible (for those who also haven't heard; the Bible is the #1 selling book in the world). From personal experience, what is known, yet still misunderstood, is Earth. It is known because it's lived on, and misunderstood because of its many mysteries. What is heaven though? Has anyone realized that heavens is plural in many versions of the Bible, yet Christian faith usually refers to heaven as one place and singular? Is heaven a place, or is it a concept? Who said these words, and who wrote the Bible? Man did! Growing up in a religious

household and going to church on a regular basis, I had a

lot of questions that could not fully be answered. It was

told to just believe what another human is saying because

they are saying it, and because they are translating from

the #1 most sold book in the world (who is selling that

book by the way?). It is not fear that drives the sales of this

text, it is the unquenchable desire to know. Religion is a

topic that can be long talked about, and is a strong

underlying force within our system. That being said, it will

not be much talked about in this book. It is the concept of

religion that must be acknowledged. There are a lot of

people of blind faith, that praise deities and those who

preach, yet know nothing of the deity or the person they

are taught by. Because they have faith in something, it's as

if it is okay to not have faith in themselves, and not fear

because their belief in their deity or their preacher. With

blind faith comes ignorance, and with that ignorance arises

that bliss. One must understand a concept becomes a

concept when more than one person believes in a certain

truth. The word certain is used because one could believe

something that they feel is wholefully true, when in fact it

is false. What is truth, and what is fallacious? This is

where the saying *"nothing is written in stone"* could come

from. Truth can vary from person to person. This is why

someone can easily pass a lie detector test if they wanted

to, because once they believe something is true, it is true to

them even tho it may in fact be false. This may be a reason

why they are no longer used in the court 'system', another

part of the corrupted world we live in. This may in fact be

the reason why we have different religions, and cultures.

The difference in truths humans hold can be seen in the

billions of books we have at our disposal. Currently in

writing is a topic, again, not the first to be known or

realized; just the first written from this perspective or truth. Do you know what your truths are, what is real, and what isn't? That is what is so beautiful about our world. We have over 7 billion people on this gorgeous planet, and no two people think exactly the same in regards to truths. How awesome is that? If this doesn't resonate with you, go have as many conversations as you can, and see if you can find one person that thinks exactly like you do. With this truth in mind, why do people blindly follow concepts? It could be because of that F word, fear. What is the biggest fear? Is it death, is it being alone, is it being wrong, or is it the fear of the unknown? Humans for so long have been trying for so long to know what their purpose is in this life, and have created an illusion derived from and fed by fear because many do not know. This fear of the unknown can be correlated directly to FOMO. Evidence to this suggestion revolves around internet usage, how quickly, and how fast information - whether true or false - can be known. People do not want to be or feel left behind in the dark of not knowing, and have a great desire to know. Fear they will be missing out on the secret to our lives is why FOMO exists, and it has been reinforced through the system we live in. Many people may fall into a place of denial or feeling that what is being said is false because this is something that they do not want to believe, yet they see it everyday, maybe even partake in it. Have you ever wondered what the first self-aware human being was like in comparison to their fellow being that wasn't? In reality, as a species, humans have lost their way of finding the path in this life. The evidence, and reflection of that is the world we live in. This is why *Systematic Desensitization* was created.

Systematic Desensitization

"If you want to go fast, go by yourself; if you want to go far, go with others"

- African Proverb

One way to strongly address FOMO, the anxiety of trying to avoid fear, what could also be seen as the fear of not knowing, or the anxiety of feeling fear itself, is a process called systematic desensitization. It is a psychological treatment used for phobias in which those in fear are progressively put into anxiety inducing moments and taught relaxation techniques in order to bypass anxiety. In layman's, if we are taught behaviors or feelings that are not able to be felt while being anxious; the feeling of being anxious is eliminated. The approach suggested is one that revolves around health, and reversing the conditioning process we've gone through. FOMO is a mental disorder, and mental health is a branch of health. The truest way to battle it goes deeper than just being in stressful situations and learning relaxation techniques. A prime example of a stressful situation is called **LIFE.** It is only stressful because we make it. This is what the Buddha try to teach. It must quickly be pointed out, in regards to counterconditioning being an animal treatment, last heard, humans are animals also. The ego has made humans feel they are above other living creatures. As human beings, we are extremely special and with that truth, it must still be known that no form of life is greater or more important than another. If this is a challenge to resonate with, think of a tree. Trees are a living life form. Without trees, we would have no oxygen, and wouldn't be able to live. Evidence of our ego arises at the will of many who are okay with cutting down copious amounts of trees. Why is it that we use the term systematic desensitization rather than the term counterconditioning? Simply put, it is because we live in a system. Because one can easily be misunderstood, you must know that the system is a whole, and it's functionality is optimally performed because of its pieces. As a human being, you are a piece within the system, because you are one of its parts, just as the trees are. Society is an entity comprised of multiple people, which means society is an organization. Organizations are as weak as their weakest link. In order to strengthen the chains that create the linkage, we must strengthen others, and this is a part of our purpose as human beings. *Systematic Desensitization* is a call to action to change the culture in which we live in so that **ALL** may thrive rather than survive. The process for this change starts with the individuals body, and their behavior that consists of people *acting* rather than *reacting*. Within this state of being, one is physically fit and able to fulfill their purpose in life, the environment they thrive in is one that not only feeds their soul, it is one in which they are a working factor in its growth. Within this state of being, each person is connected and loving to their fellow beings; all aspiring for the life we know of, yet do not see. With this environment, the mind, body, and spirit is constantly learning, growing, loving, happy, and at peace rather than in fear. This is a place where one recognizes that they truly have no control over the system we live in, it is controlled by a greater intelligence that cannot be explained nor fathomed. This is the same intelligence that keeps the heart beating, and the blood flowing. Once acknowledged, one will know that the balance beam of life is between the physical, environmental, social, mental, and spiritual branches of health. There are some people out there already living in this state of abundance, and it is your duty to help those that are not. For those not in this state, it is your duty to seek those who are. As reiterated before, our culture is currently conditioned to feel and act a certain way; in this state there is chaos, unhappiness, and decay. This is why we must counter the conditioning process derived from fear and illusions that has been instilled within people. Before working on the whole, we must work on the parts. As an organization, the whole will come together because of its parts. In order for change to be effective and successful, as a society, we must understand our current state and identify our problem. The previous chapters were meant to help guide those that needed that help. Once acknowledged, our organization must formulate a future desired state for the process of change to begin. During this stage of the process, it is up to the people to accept the responsibility, and make decisions that support the future desired state.

Once both the individual and the collective come into harmony, it creates a process known as groupthink and our system will then be able to implement a true change. Again, it is a process, and progress is an important part of this process. Make decisions that create a beautiful future, and nothing else. You have the power to see and look into the future; it begins with the light within you! In essence, your present is and will be the future. Once you let your eternal light shine as it was meant to, you will be the lighthouse that all will come to when lost. Through your social influence, a group polarization will occur, and with this polarization, balance can be achieved. We are aiming for a true culture change within the society and organization you are a part of. One change cannot happen without the other, and change begins with you.

*

www.ingramcontent.com/pod-product-compliance
Lightning Source LLC
Chambersburg PA
CBHW051349280526
45784CB00007B/2882